I0673692

ALSO FROM TELLING OUR STORIES PRESS:

REVERIE: Ultra Short Memoirs

IMPACT: An Anthology of Short Memoirs

ROLL: A Collection of Personal Narratives

TURNS: A Collection of Memoir Chapbooks

*RESURRECTING PROUST: Unearthing
Personal Narratives through Journaling*

*THE BRIDGE: A Companion Journal for
Unearthing Personal Narratives and Memoir*

SO LONG: Short Memoirs of Loss and Remembrance

MEMOIR POETIC of a NAKED COP

MY CIA: A Memoir

*EL PUENTE: Un Diario Complementario para
Descubrir Narrativas y Memorias Personales*

REFLECTIONS

Ultra Short
Personal
Narratives

REFLECTIONS

Ultra Short Personal Narratives

Collected by

CoCo Harris

TELLING OUR STORIES PRESS

Showcasing the Art of Literary Personal Narratives
Published by Telling Our Stories Press

The independent literary imprint with a focus on
the art of short memoir and personal narratives.

Requests for information should be forwarded to:
Telling Our Stories Press
www.TellingOurStoriesPress.com

Cover Art: "Self Portrait" by Vanessa Mallory Kotz
Cover Design: CoCo Harris and Michael Milliken
Book Layout: Indie Designz

Tumbling Tree ©dah / dahlusion 2015

Library of Congress Control Number: 2014916297

Printed in the United States of America
ISBN-13: 9780990008132
ISBN-10: 0990008134

This book is dedicated to
Gloria Jean Harris
and the
O-Girls

Acknowledgements

I am grateful for all of the authors who have
shared their narratives in these pages.

"To me, the most important doorway into the soul of a person is her or his words…"

—Anna Deveare Smith,
from Talk to Me: Listening Between the Lines

CONTENTS

PART 2: ROOTS **23**

ULTRA SHORT INTRODUCTION

This collection of ultra short narratives provides short snippets and reflections, which embody bits of who we are at our best, worst, and everything in between. Within these brief reminisces we have glimpses of who we've become because of, and in spite of our experiences. These flash recollections continue to tell the stories of our lives, one brief musing at a time.

Part 1:
Release

Tumbling Tree
Dah Helmer

Vision at Sixty
Larry Godwin

Born the girl to please my mom
In curly locks and dresses
I wrote my youthful chapters
Wearing Father's pants.

I breathed love that smothered
And when she left
I searched for other bosoms
To shield me from slurs and bruises.

I married young, my mother's twin,
And promptly became her ward –
Cinched up Father's belt another notch
And camped at her feet.

I'll meet my death among brothers
In a cabin fashioned by my own hands
Wrapped in a writhing blizzard
Rejoicing: I was enough.

Solar Electric Voyage in the Ocean Rowboat Morocco—1991
Kathleen Saville

We stood glaring at each other. Neither of us giving in. He wanted me to go. But I refused to motor across the Atlantic in our old ocean rowboat, re-outfitted with extra solar panels and a trolling motor. Taking our young son on Excalibur was crazy.

All the coastal and lake trials had not convinced me. Excalibur was only an ocean rowboat and not an oceangoing solar-electric-motor boat.

The voyage failed. Six months later, with our ocean rowboat abandoned where he had started the solar trip alone, I returned to school to begin my own journey alone.

A Child's Vision
Susan White

I was four, maybe five, living in our 3-bedroom ranch house.

Our television— the one that stopped turning on—lay on the trampled ground of our side yard, its screen facing the milky, November sky. I planted my red sneakers in a wide, parallel stance and looked down at her plasma womb that arched toward the muffled sun.

The virginal, merry mother, miraculously begetting characters to save us from pain and boredom,

Lay on her back atop the yellowed clumps of grass . . .awaiting Father to take her to the dump behind the market.

My trembling, skinny arms released the large rock I'd carried from the corner of our sparse vegetable garden. I prayed for the stories' characters to arise: Bugs Bunny, Kermit, Gilligan, and the good, pretty, nose-twitching witch.

I believed, I believed, I believed.
I opened my eyes to a dark, noxious cloud—no white stallion galloping out of the rupture—and I choked on the fumes of fact.

Life Support
Elayne Clift

She awoke, and wondered again
how many days would pass
before the sound of the slap
was no longer her rising image.

She thought it sounded like
the Titanic crashing into that iceberg,
the rapid snap tearing her in two
like the bow of the once indestructible ship.

Later, when she knew that the
fissure was not of her making,
but had come from a fractured and frail mind,
she rejected anger, replaced it with stoic silence.

But the sting was there, still and forever,
their long affection now on life-support.
And having neither the courage nor the will
to pull the plug, she simply endured her loss,
quietly and alone, awaiting the next blow.

People in Paper Gowns
Jasminne Mendez

When you're in /a hospital gown/you are not a teacher. /Or a writer /or an actress /or a poet /or anyone special. /You/ are a patient. /You have no social status/and your humility /and/or ego /is irrelevant. /You are a lab rat. /As unnecessary /as the joke /the nurse makes/to try/ and make you feel "comfortable". /In a faded paper gown /you may/as well /be naked /on a freeway. /Stripped from your persona/you lie on a cold /hard hospital bed /clinging to the only/shred of dignity /you have left /which hangs /miserably on the unintentional "thank you" /that escapes from your mouth/as the doctor hurriedly /leaves the room. /You don't have a right /to ask questions in the gown. /No you have to be fully/dressed /before you can do that. /You cannot pretend /to be modest /about your lopsided breasts /and hairy knees /because your sudden /imperfections /won't change the test results. /And being comfortable /or anything more positive /than anxious /would make you seem/ arrogant./Because /in a hospital gown /you are just sir or ma'am /and I'm sorry and /I hope that doesn't hurt. /Nameless. /Shameless. /A forgotten face /in a pile of folders/that will only /be remembered /if you're asked/to come back /and do it /all /over /again.

My Daughter's Exoskeleton
Nicole L. V. Mullis

Sometimes, I do a double take when my oldest daughter enters the room. She is ten, nearly eleven, and her features are more beautiful than cute. When I brush her hair—which isn't often anymore—I'm the one standing on a stool.

When she was a toddler, she had a favorite blanket called "Blan." She dressed it in her brother's baby clothes, fed it bottles and took it for walks. It looked awful, like she was playing with a decapitated doll. One day, my mother coaxed it from her and turned it into a real doll.

"Blan Baby" has been there in sickness and in health all the days of my daughter's life. My daughter adores her but times are changing. She worries her friends will find out she sleeps with a doll and now hides her inside the pillowcase. Yet, during a recent bout of bronchitis, Blan Baby was out of the pillowcase and pillowing my daughter's fevered head.

Years of loyalty have left their mark. Blan Baby's paper-thin fabric is coming apart. My mother offered to recover her. My husband jokingly referred to it as an exoskeleton. We laughed but my daughter balked, "How will I know she's really in there?"

Such sweet sentiment from a girl who, two nights earlier, rolled her eyes and said, "Dad, I'm ten years old. I can handle a knife!"

Exoskeleton or not, I know the doll's days are numbered. Cute boys, curfews, driving a car and choosing a college will consume what's left of girlhood. Already it is easier to see the adult my daughter will be than the baby she was. Sometimes I worry if she's really in there.

Stepping In and Out
Fran Tempel

Saddle shoes: What other shoe could possibly describe the bane of my youth? These white shoes with a black "saddle" over the middle and black heels topped off with black laces crisscrossing through eight sliver eye holes were indestructible.

Growing up in a large family, with never ending hand-me-downs, the only brand new item we were each assured of would be a pair of shoes. I knew not to expect ruby-red or glass slippers, but I always held out hope of something different. But these shoes would wear like iron and only need replacing when outgrown. For years I felt as a convict might, wearing the same unchanging outfit. "Well," Mom would say in response to my complaints, "When you make your own money you can buy what you want."

So I did!

After cashing my first paycheck as a freshman, I sprinted to the store to feast on all the wonderful possibilities. I selected a pair of mahogany colored penny loafers. Seeing my feet emancipated from those cement-looking contraptions filled me with delight.

Then I spotted a pair of pointed-toe, three-inch black heels. It was love at first touch: soft, pliant—utterly feminine! Sliding my feet into them, I was overtaken by an astonishingly new sensation: at once sensuous and sensual. They caressed my feet; I was breathless. In the mirror I was shocked to suddenly see that my calves had morphed into a womanly shape. I stood mesmerized.

In that moment I visualized the endless possibilities when I left this store, this town, this state, making plans that only those who are set free are able to do.

Horizon
Judith Ellen

My childhood ended sometime between three p.m. and sunset. I had been running effortlessly (I was a fast girl) to go catch the sun. I saw its distinct line fading in the distance. I quickened my pace only to stop abruptly at its edge. The sunlight, whose trail I had followed, disappeared, and all that remained was darkness. I was scared. I had stumbled into an unfamiliar place of lockers, angst, mascara, and pep rallies.

I fearlessly traded in my Buster Browns for pumps.

Original Crip
Notty Bumbo

See, I'm an Original Crip - a natural-born cripple, dig? And not as props or anything, but just to show how long I have been "exposed" to these awful realities: when I was a kid, 5 or so, I spent lots of time at a clinic for other crips like me, and my first girl friend, if you will, was a black girl with no arms. We used to ride the rocking horse together, and I recall those as the better times in that setting, better by far than my home life. One day, on the way home, I recall my father asking my mother why I was always playing with those "n****s", and while I did not understand the word yet, I immediately got the tone and the intent, and that was the start of learning about my fathers racism, which sometimes pored out of him like a flood. We became estranged by the time I was ten or so, and have not actually communicated in more than 30 years, for which I feel no regrets at all. And despite many years in the 60s and 70s working best I knew how to counter its manifestations whenever I encountered it, I find it beyond repulsive we are still having to do this work. So I vacillate between rage and despair, cynicism and righteous indignation, and often have to fall back on sarcasm and silly humor just to stay in the fight.

Sweet Story
Jeannette Drake

(for the Mother Emanuel Nine)

I lace my lemonade
with honey, instead
of white sugar
like daddy did. This pitcher,
only half a fix.
"Nobody knows the trouble
I've seen. Glory!"
Behind closed doors thunder rises
until a three year old refuses
to speak her violator's name
(the way people refuse to whisper
Dyllan Roof.)
Instead, for fifty-odd years
I watch Hop-a-long Cassidy,
Wild Bill Hickok, the Cisco Kid.
Who are these gunslingers
and brown bandits
with silky shoulder length hair?
Nightly, I plead; pray
for long braids, not blue eyes.
I do not forget galloping horses,
Indian braves, dust storms in the desert,
slamming doors or empty mayonnaise
jars that crash against walls after midnight.

I close my eyes. Now lay me down
to sleep, my soul to keep in a cool green forest.
Monarch butterflies and honeysuckle tickle
my nose. Pink mimosa float through haunted houses.
Fireflies flicker along windowpanes until
a stranger appears with nail prints in his feet.
He hands me a list with names of berserk cowboys
and a cup of lemonade.

Meat Loaf
Maryann Gremillion

It doesn't sprout wings on my tongue.
My mother's, out of the oven, crisp in the pan meatloaf is not my
favorite color, reeks with white onions, like tiny eyes in mud, is a
slice of brick on my plate, with tomato sauce dripping into the
mashed potatoes, a bloody river—and I have to eat it because the
recipe is from Betty Crocker.

I watch my mother's iron face chew in hard silence. When her eyes
collapse within themselves, I cover the meat with a paper towel,
walk across the linoleum and dump it in the trash—I never liked
meat loaf, and now I can say so.

No Shame
C. A. Davis

It's unfortunate that I was molested, raped, and abused by my stepmother because I looked too much like my mother, and that I lied to people about the cause of death of my father.

It's also unfortunate that my father tried to take my mother with him because he wanted to take his big secret to the grave —and she threatened to tell all. What secret so big?
He was married with children, but loved money enough to sleep with wealthy men. The secret didn't make it to his grave because on 9/11/02 as he died of AIDS, my family decided to fill me in.

I should be angry, demand answers, hate the world, but I'm not.

MAY 8, 2015
S. F. Siddiqui

Five years ago I bought a Conair hair trimmer to remove my newborn's hair. Today, I used that trimmer to shave off my mother's.

She asked me to do it yesterday. When I arrived today, prepared, she lowered her loosely-draped scarf. Though I knew what to expect, I was surprised by how much of her pink scalp showed from beneath the sparse, stringy hair, how small and overwhelmed she looked, beaten by weeks of infusions and pills.

I rolled a chair in front of the bathroom sink. She sat down and crossed her arms on the basin, then rested her head on her forearms. As she sat slumped over like that, I methodically worked the trimmer through to make sure no uneven clumps remained. I was nervous about how she would react upon seeing the finished product. I worried she would see her own father in the reflection and remembered his cancer was discovered too late for treatment. I knew she would not let herself reveal any vain disappointment at the loss of her hair, and yet I wondered what feelings she would keep hidden.

Halfway through, I realized this was taking too long, and I asked her if I should keep going. She shrugged, eyes closed. I could not remember another time I had seen her patiently sit still. There were no instructions, no list of expectations. Just the dull buzz of the machine.

When I finished, I busied myself in clearing away the clumps of hair that littered the sink and bathroom floor, the strays stubbornly sticking to her shoulders. She helped too, then glanced quickly at the mirror.

She looked beautiful. Cool. I hadn't expected that. The salt-and-pepper spikes. The dark, direct gaze. The straight, strong back.

That's what happens when you take back control.

I Am My Father's Daughter
Sharine Aupke

Like most child parent relationships, my father and I stumbled through tough times together hoping to find the happy place at the end of the road. Although, the greatest lesson I learned from my father was after his passing three years ago.

We were both stubborn. He was a blues musician for most of his life and this made him tough on the outside. The last time I spoke with him was three months before his passing as my grandmother passed and he had the task of calling to inform me. I was at work when he called. He was upset, angry, bitter, and sad. Despite knowing that my grandmother had been battling illness for quite some time, I did not take the news well. During the conversation, my father voiced his opinion on a couple of things and I took offense to it. I was blinded by my own sadness and not recognizing that he was suffering as well when I rebutted with some words of resentment towards him. After we hung up I decided not to speak to him for a while allowing him time to cool down. In March, his best friend showed up at my place of business. When I asked how my father was: "Oh honey, I thought you knew…" I learned that he had passed on Valentines Day.

Over the last three years, I have come to terms with his death. I realized that he had taught me the final lesson he was ever going to teach me in life: That "I am sorry," are the most powerful words on the planet.

Dealing with Life
Laurence Snydal

When the time comes to cover the last bet,
You shove your stack of chips out in the pile.
You check your cards once more and then you smile.

But no one gets just what they hoped to get.
Opening, raising, calling, cruel fates,
And then a friendless fellowship of doom,
And poker faces in a smoke-filled room.

Still maybe you could avoid aces and eights,
The dead man's hand, and fill your inside straight
To rake in the pot that's called forever.
At any rate, ante up or never
See what the dealer dealt.

I tempted fate.

Fate gave me a queen of hearts and a pair
Of kings. I've held them close to my heart since.
I'll cover but I won't raise. I convince
Myself I have the best hand anywhere.
And it's true. I need no more cards. I'm done.
Life is a game I've already won.

Part 2: Roots

Traveling Down Roots
Jane Falla

Listening to his deep-rooted rage, my mind wanders.
Waking up in Munich, rushing to the train in blackness; then
Budapest, escaping a one-night stand.

In Prague, everything blue, then back in Germany, everything
green. In England, all gray, except for hazy gold when I see Chris,
like meeting in Australia, and all I want to do is kiss him, hard and
slow.

In Amsterdam, stoned, hung over, grateful for brown, toast and the
cozy hostel.

In Singapore, wading through whites in aisles of the orchid garden.
At the zoo, looking through silver bars, birds insistently flapping.

Fast forward, red, caged myself, trying so hard to fly.

Cristina Joy
Anika H. Klix

For the last time, I made the journey across the water by ferry. It was early morning and the fog was rolling in off Puget Sound. As I looked out across the bay, tears welled up in my eyes. For the last time I would step foot inside my mother's home. Memories of Thanksgiving dinners, weekend getaways, cooking, and watching musicals with the children while Mom and I sang loudly out of tune; the kids laughing and rolling their eyes.

For the last time, I walked through the empty rooms, artwork and interior decorations packed away to take back with me. Cristina Joy was beautiful, talented, cheerful, creative, amazing, artistic...In fact, she lived and breathed ART. Everything she touched was artistic; from her "Corn silks" clothing designs, to fashions she altered from her closet or found at the local thrift shop, to her home decor. Re-upholstered, re-purposed, and re-cycled furniture; artwork she created, re-painted, re-framed, or fashioned out of fabric and Mod Podge. Mundane re-usable grocery bags up-cycled with colorful fabric and unique buttons; I cherish every single one. I will always remember how passionately she danced. Her choreography spoke to my soul, everyone's soul who saw her. Tina, pretty ballerina.

For the last time, so many years ago as a young child, I remember making May Day baskets with construction paper, filling them with bluebells and dandelions to hang on the front door. I'd knock loudly, run and hide behind the porch and wait for her to answer...she'd smile...and I loved her.

My mother died on May 1, 2013 from cancer and on that day, for the first time, May Day flowers hung on Heaven's door.

Black and White Photograph of Your Mother

Judith Serin

It's three-and-a-half by five; you know because you just bought the frame. Taken in England, you think. She looks young--thirties? forties? —and at first you think her hair is pulled back but then see it's short. Why does the baby fine hair you have in common look so full? Her forehead is much higher than yours. She's in three-quarters profile, a pose that flattered you at that age too. Her jaw-line is strong, her large nose not noticeable.

A man in dark pants and white shirt walks toward her down the tree-lined avenue, the trees in metal cages that repeat the spikes of an old iron railing behind her. She wears a cardigan, a dark top under it, the handles of her purse looped casually over her arm. She sits on the edge of a brick walled flowerbed, the old houses behind her covered in ivy. How you want to enter there.

Peete's Wedge
Carl Whitehead, Jr

The reason I wanted to play golf was because I saw Calvin Peete on my godmother's Technicolor television set. He was a dark skinned man wearing a white Kango cap, a white golf shirt, in a sea of green, green grass flooding the background and there he was, walking with confidence. I know he was not the first black man to play on the PGA, but he was the first one I saw. Prior to seeing him play, I was never interested in the game. When I started to follow his career I understood his significance to the game as well as to others before him.

Years ago, I purchased a right handed Calvin Peete wedge, even though I am left handed, just to have it. I was able to obtain a few autograph items as well. However, I did not get to meet the man. My loss. Thank you Mr. Peete.

Cabbage Days
Susan Mahan

(In Memory of Dad 5/5/05)

A whiff of sauerkraut at a food court
brought back memories
of Saturday night suppers in South Boston
before I was ten years old:

hot dogs, baked beans
and brown bread for Mum and us kids,
a side of sauerkraut for Dad.

I couldn't fathom Dad's choice,
but, then, he was mostly a mystery to me.
He spent a lot of time reading
and had a far-off look in his eyes
when he glanced up from his books--
two traits I eventually acquired.
I now know that he traveled the world from his armchair.

Mickey Survives
Robert M. Shafer

At my birth, Dad declared me a bastard and cruelly nicknamed me Blondie. Luckily he abandoned our family when I turned five. When I was seven, Mom gave me to well-meaning strangers. In 1951, when I turned nine, Mom found a new home for me by posting an ad in a Chicago newspaper. The brutal woman she gave me to wanted a child slave. I lived in bondage to Naomi for the next four years. When I was twelve, she died from a stroke. My good luck again. I feared she would kill me during one of her violent rages.

Uncle Charlie, Handsome Fella
Pamela Gay

> *Aye, it's a story alright.*
> *—in the spirit of James Kelmen*

"Without our stories we'd have nothing," a dying father says to a daughter in a memoir she was reading, but what she heard was her father interrupting with an impatient "yeah yeah" whenever someone asserted some belief or went on too long like Uncle Charlie "handsome fella" (he taught us kids to say) when he came to visit and entertained us with stories of sports cars and women, where he'd been, where he was headed now, and "remember when" he'd say to my mother who hadn't gone anywhere since then when…but that's another story.

It's All Relative
Shirlee Sky Hoffman

Two grandmothers and my mother
Four generations--skipping one--
On my hall wall
Eye-level
I have eyed them each time I pass
For years now
And as the years pass
They grow younger
Before my eyes,
The two grandmothers.

Not my mother.
She stays the same,
A wispy-haired, timid mite
In the middle
Of her old age on her left
And Aunt Rose's old age on her right.

Over time, as I go by,
My eyes have come to notice
We are gradually converging,
My great great grandmother
My great grandmother
And me,
Until I may have already met and bypassed the younger.

Winging on,

I move at unbelievable velocity

(Who could have convinced me how fast life passes?)
Toward overcoming the elder as well.

Under the Peonies
Dawn Marie Thompson

The screaming goes on and on.

I hide under the porch, curled in a ball on the dirt, holding my ears.

The screaming dissolves into a long, low howl. Then it stops, replaced by sounds of shuffling back and forth, creaking floorboards.

Time passes. Above me, the screen door slams. I peek out from between the slats. My father, carrying two bundles wrapped in what looks like towels or cotton pillowcases, comes down the porch steps and walks across the front lawn to the tangled flower garden that sprawls along the fence separating the farmhouse from the pasture beyond. Setting the two parcels down on the grass, he picks up a shovel and digs a hole at each end of the garden, beneath two bushes that bookend it. The bushes droop with huge, heavy pink blossoms that seem to look down at what he's doing.

He picks up the two white bundles and bends to place one in each of the waiting depressions. One in, two in. He shovels soft, back earth over both. One covered, two covered. He tosses the shovel down and turns back to the house.

I scuttle back into my hiding place, viciously sucking my thumb. He mounts the steps, crosses the porch over my head and enters the house. I stop sucking. I hear his low voice over the sobbing of his wife: "I took care of them. They're under the peonies."

Village Accent
Yuan Changming

Growing up in lianhuadang (a remote Chinese village)
I have never gotten rid of my grotesque country accent
Even since I began to speak Mandarin
As those in big cities or on television can

While attending college in Shanghai, I felt deeply hurt
Each time a teacher or classmate made fun of my dialect
But inside of my own home, I feel truly delighted
Whenever my wife or son imitates my English speech act

To make myself sound less foreign in a foreign land
I often hope to wear a mask covering my voice print
Like a big soil-colored birthmark near my mouth
Or perhaps, to have a tattoo formed around this area

Backslidin'
Jade Banks

Every now and then
I slip into my old mode of thinking

> *That light means beautiful...*
> *That thin means attractive...*

It usually happens when a pretty man shows me some attention.
Then, the twenty years of my earlier conditioning overcome my
past five years of hard work.

So, I put up with his flaws and his ignorance and his lack of
ambition because he looks good on my arm.

Nothing like a good-looking man
> *to up the status of a woman*
> *aesthetically in debt...*

I pray to God that he can fuck, so I can have an excuse for keeping
him around (one that I convince myself is legitimate).

Long Road to China
Danielle Stonehirsch

The sun was already hot on the beach, and the sand burned. My grandparents watched me while my parents took a walk. Bored after only ten minutes, I paced in short ovals, kicking up sand as I went. My grandfather, captain of my world, sat up in his chair long enough to say, "I want you to dig me a hole to China. Then we can pop over together." This sounded like a lot of work, but if my grandfather wanted to see China, then my whole life's purpose was about to be dedicated to digging to China. He told me the best place to start and handed me my blue shovel.

I was digging when my parents came back, but they didn't disturb me. They were happy to see me engaged at a reasonable distance. I kept digging a larger and larger hole around myself, until lunchtime. I wouldn't leave my hole, so a sandwich was handed down to me. The top of the hole was already higher than my shoulders.

I paid no attention to my family talking as I dug my way further to the center of the earth. But as the sun started to set, my mother came to take me home. I was desperate. I sat in my hole and refused to leave and screamed as my father pulled me out and dragged me across the sand towards civilization. My family was shocked. It took awhile before I was able to stop crying long enough to explain how greatly I'd failed my grandfather. My mother whirled on my surprised grandfather, who had long forgotten his request. I hugged my father as he carried me farther and farther from my half finished hole, knowing my grandfather and I would never see China together.

You Can Handle the Truth
Michelle Ardillo

"Who has the Dunkin' Donuts document? Where is the lease brief for the Dunkin' Donuts document? FedEx says it was delivered last Thursday." Thus began an otherwise innocuous day at work as a real estate paralegal in 1988. My boss, the towering six-foot tall general counsel of the firm, often referred to as the barracuda, was tearing through our department, shouting and searching for this missing document, with the vice-president of leasing on her heels. Being new, I cowered in my tiny cubicle, head down, clicking away on my computer.

Later, as I was cleaning off my desk to go home, I moved a stack of files and, to my great horror, there was the infamous Dunkin' Donuts document. I had had it all along. Panic ensued while different scenarios, all involving lies, played in my head. After a few minutes, I remembered something my father had told me when I left home for my first real job after college: "Always tell the truth. If you screw up, you be the one to tell your boss. Don't let them hear it from someone else." So, I marched to her office and told her I had had the document all along, that it had been buried on my desk. I apologized profusely and said, "What would you like me to do now?" She just glared at me and finally, after an eternity, said, "Can you draft it now and get it out by FedEx tomorrow?"

The next day she complimented me for coming to her with the truth. I went on to tell her it was one of many lessons he had taught me about honesty and having a strong work ethic. Thanks, Daddy.

Crab Meat
Paul Hedella

Jill jumped down from the windowsill, rubbed against our legs, and then gobbled a whole can of the food that my brother spooned into her dish. "Poor thing was starving," Frank reported to mom back at our apartment. "Probably would have eaten another can of that crab meat, but Miss Sheridan only left enough for one a day."

"Crab meat?!" mom boomed, in that duck-for-cover voice of hers. "Surely you're mistaken."

We had to march upstairs to Miss Sheridan's apartment and show her, because she wouldn't believe us.

"This is not right," she said, when she saw the proof sitting there on the kitchen counter. She grabbed the cans and took them back to our apartment. Then she disappeared out the door and returned twenty minutes later with a bag from Roy's up the street. It was full of regular cat food.

"Twenty-four cents a can," she said. "In comparison, do you have any idea what crab meat costs?"

Frank and I fed Jill "savory shreds of beef" the rest of the week, while mom ate crab. After the second day, she stopped telling us we should try it. Frank and I weren't interested. Jill was a sweet white cat with one green eye and one blue. She hadn't meant to make mom angry. Mom was just touchy about some things, especially when it came to money. If strangers knocked on our door, selling magazines or some miracle cleaning spray, mom would treat them rudely.

"Believe it or not, we're poor," she would say, before shutting the door firmly in their faces.

Front Yard: Act I
Jennifer Higgins

It is something that stays with you all your life— the moment something unthinkable happens to a creature you adore. He's an imposing 5 foot 10. Hands as rough as the hewn wood with which he works. His white t-shirt and flannel over shirt small of Mennen speed stick, which is the only cologne he owns. Anger is so much a part of his life that it has shaped his physical self. The anger is most evident in his gaze, a mixture of serene sky blue and unbridled insanity. And it's not just the alcohol he's imbibed, because his craziness lasts the whole daylong.

It was a cool, clear autumn day in the mid-1970's. I stood several paces behind father, outside in our fenced-in front yard. Leaves had begun to line the Goshen stone front steps. His anger came suddenly at this moment. I felt her small, furry gray and black tiger pelt pass before my feet. I was aware that father saw her too. His eyes fixed on her svelte form. I recall the way he cruelly grabbed Pussin, held her low in front of his foot and then kicked with a force I couldn't then fathom. He kicked her like a football and she flew up into the air like one too. She then fell hard on the ground and sprinted away. I wished I could've followed Pussin, left this angry man forever. What I would do was vow. Vow never to replicate this angry man's detestable actions. This is the moment when I learned at once that people can commit egregious acts but that other people have the power not to.

Part 3: Trajectories

Shoes
Victoria Brott

As an infant I wore slippers

As a toddler I wore sturdy supportive leather shoes

As a preteen I wore flip-flops

As a teenager I wore pointed high heels

As a young woman of the sixties, I wore rings on my toes and

bracelets on my ankles, barefooted and independently free

As a working woman I wore pointed high heels

As an older woman I wore flip-flops

As a grandmother I wore sturdy supportive leather shoes

As a retired grandmother I wear slippers.

I Bought a Stranger a $5 Dress
Jas Mardis

I was recently looking for a dress for my grown daughter and wound up buying one for a complete stranger.

When my daughter was a girl I bought all of her dresses…and bows…and shoes…and rounds of skeet ball at the game arcades around Dallas. We had a five-dollar limit. When the arcades started closing I wanted to show her that we could have fun on that same five dollars at other places, too. After trying her eight year old's ideas, I made a suggestion that we try to find a piece of clothing. It didn't take long for that ridiculous idea to become a family bet. We would pick an outlet store and each enter with only a $5 bill. We had one hour to find a piece of clothing, it had to fit, and had to be worn one day the following week. We called it The Five Dollar Run.

So, recently I was in one such store when I noticed a young lady watching me flip through the rack of dresses and select a few for my cart. After a little bit she walked over and said that I was picking the wrong sizes if I was shopping for myself. We laughed…I more than her. I told her about the FIVE DOLLAR RUN and she didn't miss a beat and checked the prices of the items in my cart. She was impressed and within thirty minutes wanted to join in.

We shopped and talked about my daughter and why I wasn't buying dresses for a wife instead. It was a pretty good time for the next half hour or so until she spotted something and asked me to meet her at the dressing rooms in five minutes. At the dressing rooms she was holding up a pair of boots with missing laces and a scratch on the left toe. She asked if the scratch was acceptable then laughed and slapped me on the shoulder when I showed her the dress with the missing belt and loop.

HOARSE
Jamie Brunson

Who Flying Woman was first
OR How She became Hoarse

SMALL BLOOD-WET THING BURSTING AND HOPING
eyes fall open on this ole worl
then

GIRL LEAPING
shied plaited/pigtailed pulsing like rainwater
kicking high panty less
then

PLACED WOMAN
bloodied laid flat in a crawl space missing her knees
counting splits and scratching
then

DISAPPEARING WOMAN FROM INCOMPLETENESS
smelling air through cracks swallowing it hard shaking the box
loudly uncashed Her
receiving tunnel smells sweetly scent wafts a head turns lid
dislodges stark light
thaws eyes
then

—let wobbly

made to prance
caged reigned belled
snorting while patted elegant feet
shoed—
HOARSE

Beach Glass
Bonnie J. Morris

I was the gifted child. Tested, rated, praised. I was always the youngest, the achiever, skipped ahead, head buried in a book.

Then I became the aging precocious, as awkward as a colt. Yes, ten books, but no bestseller; professor, yet untenured, due to economic shifts in academe. And critics jeered, How come you're not rich, if you're such a genius?

I walked on life's beaches. I collected beach glass, those bright imperfect pieces tumbling smoothly back to us. I became a bright imperfect piece; I landed, happy, on my lovers' towels; I wrote, in ink, in consonants and vowels.

My Life Story
Gerald Harris

Poor boy

Smart kid

Gets noticed

Takes risks

Wins some

Loses Some

Loves Often

Hurts Sometimes

Grows old

Gives thanks

Poem
Giuseppe Infante

It's 3:58 a.m. in my back yard.
Bird is chirping.
Is it the same bird that eats my grass-seed?
"Where are you?"
No other birds are chirping.
It must be lonesome being stuck in a tree.
I always wanted a tree house.
I don't like steak too much, I'd rather have a hamburger.
I love chicken, and wonder what quail tastes like.
Rabbit is a good mix of beef and chicken, I've had it twice.
Bird is chirping.
Where are all the other birds?
Brooklyn is muggy in my flannel
The bic is empty
The bowl is empty
Mosquitoes are biting
My hands are itching
The bird is still chirping
"Where are you?"
It's 4:03 a.m.
My skin is cracking
The brightness is dimming
And I have 4% left.
All my peers are traveling and writing
I make babies

From China's Village of Red Stone Bridge to San Francisco's Golden Gate Bridge
Jing Li

My desperate mother tried but failed to abort me by pushing a heavy wooden washboard against her stomach, and jumping violently. At the age of two months, she left me, in the hands of my illiterate peasant grandmother who had bound feet, firecracker temper, and once tossed her own newborn baby into the toilet like a used diaper because it was a girl.

I miraculously survived, like "a born stubborn dog" as Grandmother would call me, the world's worst man-made famine by the Chinese Communist Government in 1959–1962, after they ate all the tree leaves and grass when forty-five million peasants died of starvation.

By eight years old in my parents' one-room city apartment, I was a servant and maid to my two brothers. By age ten, I had cheated death four times. When my own daughter was born, my father-in-law pressured me to kill my baby so as to try for a boy.

I triumphed over all the curve balls life threw at me. Besides special angels appearing to rescue me at every crucial turning point of my life, education is my sanctuary. Nothing was able to crush my spirit of loving school, hardworking and excelling. Through fierce academic competitions, I went on to China's best language university, became an achieving high school teacher and eventually earned my Master's degree in America.

My hard life has taught me basic survival skills and to spend carefully and budget wisely. I'm enjoying my sweet American dream as a San Francisco homeowner and high school teacher, respected and loved by my students. My heart ripples with ecstasy every time I think about my baby daughter's life I spared, the Rice University and MBA graduate.

Mama, I Hope Your Wishes Were Granted
Vincent J. Tomeo

Mama you wanted to live in a cottage
not a basement below the level of the floor

Mama you wanted to have a happy home
but papa left you

And your two sons died

Mama you wanted to keep your feet warm
and be buried with your slippers on
but the funeral director returned them

Timehop
Crystal Wilkinson

Timehop: May 9, 1979. I am 16 years old and preparing to graduate from high school. My grandmother says I wear too much blue stuff around my eyes. I want to wear crop tops and halter tops but I am a bit too shy. My wooden soled Candy shoes are my favorites. My favorite word is beaucoup. I will live off Campbell's tomato soup and cheese and mayo sandwiches that summer because I want to be thin for college. I have been corresponding with a boy I met in freshman orientation by letter. He thinks I am going be his girlfriend when we get to campus. He will send me pictures of himself in sky blue suits all summer--prom, church. I will feel guilty for all of my young adult life for not reciprocating his crush. He will become famous in the gospel music world. He will become gay. Of course he was gay then but he would have never said that. I lament the fact that we could have been great friends and helped each other avoid 15 years of chaos. I wish him bliss. I hope he is happy.

Her
CarrZa DuBose

And I say to you people do not call her that.

She had left here a whore!

Made claims to return a maiden wearing an old hat and possessing the eyes of a hundred years before.

I tell you saints do not call her that which she claims.

Can't you see? The same Sarah born nineteen hundred and fifty nine, right here in this very congregation. Sat right there in that pew looking as innocent as a white Eve before she knew the death of knowledge and before she opened herself up for men to take her. Sad shame. Her mama and the elders spoke of a prophetess. She was struck in the head by a cross set on fire by the Klan, so you tell me if she is what she claims.

Five-year Plan
Michelle LeGault

My family is like the Brady Bunch in every way except for the perfect smiles, parents who love each other and kids who enjoy "family time." There are six of us kids. We're loud. We're rude. It's chaotic, always. Our dog ate a hole in the carpet once. Then he ate his collar. This, among other things, forced me to move out, on my own dime, against my better judgment.

I earned a four-year degree that I don't use. I married a writer and moved to Minneapolis. We have a house, a dog named Mackinac, a live-in brother/pseudo-son-child and we go to the same church as just about every twenty-something in the metro area. On holidays my husband and I drive to Michigan and dream of touring the U.S. living in an R.V. motor home.

That is our five-year plan.

Trials to Triumph
Katrenia Busch

Here is a story about a girl, many know well

If you haven't heard yet, sit back and I'll tell

She was overlooked, not acknowledged, the last to be sought

A complete outcast from the world, in which she fought

Fought to be wanted either at home or at school

For a refuge anywhere, sought an exception to the rule

She felt hated, ignored, was thrown to the side

She was a girl, without a friend, or anyone to confide

Raised by drug addicts, a young witness to violence and crime

Just a poor girl, from the ghetto….. Wasn't worth anyone's time

With a father in prison and a mother on dope

She was rescued by the state, but left without hope

She kept the hurt and pain deep inside

Tears falling, alone in a place she could hide

As she lay awake all night, praying from her bed

She slept with the blanket, pulled over her head

A girl who's been broken, ripped and torn apart

Was never given a chance, even from the start

She was stubborn, hardworking and far too proud

Fake pity from anyone, not something she allowed

An angry Goth chick, always in black

Motivated to get out, and never look back

Everyone told her, she will never be anything, nor become

Something of worthy, because of where she's from

Broke and homeless age sixteen

Seeking her diploma, only a vision seen

On the outside, only looking through

Envying others, and the love they knew

A dream she held for many years

To succeed in life, a motivator among peers

She's a girl, able to lead……..by taking a stand

Living proof to the nobodies throughout the land

She dared to be different, embraced the struggles and strife

Transformed them from pain to valuable lessons in life

Stronger and wiser, she has really grown

Came back fighting from the depths she was thrown

Turning all problems, into hope that's gained

From leaning to God, the one who remained

A girl who came from nowhere, that conquered raging seas

Climbed many mountains, some call her nurse, friend and mommy

She spends her time reading, both day and night

Where many others find darkness, she finds light

A girl who turned her many fears and countless tears

Into motivation to succeed throughout the years

A girl with courage, marches to beat of her own drum

Alive with hope and provides inspiration to some

At the Acton Council on Aging Senior Center
Michael Estabrook

On the wall above the metal rack filled with helpful magazines and pamphlets about wheelchairs, lifting devices, and mechanized beds, an insignificant yet surprisingly loud little clock is tick tick ticking away every second I sit squirming on this dented metal folding chair in the waiting area smelling of must and mice and decaying yellow flowers.

I'm here for my appointment with Mary Jane the Medicare expert because as anyone who has ventured within a light year of Medicare knows, without an expert to guide you it is impossible to begin to understand this impenetrable bureaucratic tar pit.

Suddenly, sitting here listening to that fucking clock, I panic. I want to bolt from these rooms of looming death. How did I get here in the first place? How did I ever get to be so damned old? If I leave right now I'll be able to reverse time and return to my girlfriend's parent's living room or in the hall outside her homeroom in Building Seven or in her Hofstra University dorm lobby where she will appear, radiant and resplendent in her vibrant youth and beauty and in the promise of life everlasting. I didn't mind waiting one bit back then. I would have waited until the end of time for her if necessary.

PART 4: Defining Moments

Showtime Con Timbolina
Andres Cisneros

Another Failed Attempt
Vanessa Mallory Kotz

Nearly an entire bottle of prescription-strength antihistamine topped off with three benzos for luck. A heartfelt note begging forgiveness and trying, in vain, to describe my suffering. Then blackout. I heard later that I fell from the bed to the floor, breathing but completely unresponsive. My husband stayed with me, holding me, reading to me, watching my slow breaths in and out. They did not find the note. His brother, eating cereal as he stood over my body said I was drunk and would be fine. His confused, elderly parents tried to get me back into bed, put ice on my neck, but did not call 911. What would the neighbors think? Then doctors yelling, poking me with needles and a catheter. What did you take!? I try to speak but nothing comes out. Blackness welcomes me back into its arms. Then it's all over. I'm awake. I'm alive. I feel like I could jog around the block. Fuck. I thought I'd really gotten it right this time... damn it to hell. I see David asleep, cramped into a terrible pretzel in the chair next to my bed in ICU. I see the clock. It's nearly ten. "David, don't miss your dentist appointment." He startles awake as if the cat just asked for a glass of milk.

"Self Portrait" by Vanessa Mallory Kotz

Reborn
Jason Irwin

A man in a green mask
asked me to count
backwards from one
hundred. At ninety-eight
the table began to spin;
I thought I was being swallowed
by the light
that hung above me
like giant insect eyes.

I could mark time
by the surgeries; the way
my grandmother marked
my growth
with pencil slashes
on her kitchen doorframe.

Each time I awoke
from that abyss
where God refused to dwell—
my mouth a desert;
my eyes two stones
sunk in my skull—
some small part of me
had died, some
small part was reborn.

Garbage Moon
Ashley Duran

On long car rides home, we would lie awake in the dark. From the back seat of our station wagon, we listened to our parent's whisper, the words somehow distorted and fuzzy by the time it reached our ears. Our child eyes looked for our garbage moon, bobbing in between the trees, the one that glowed behind curdled clouds.

We knew the garbage moon would take us home, eventually. We let ourselves drift into the warmness of sleep. And each time, my father carried us into the house one by one, while we pretended not to be awake.

My father drives home alone now; the garbage moon follows silently beside him. In my mind I can hear his breathing catch, as he gets out of the car and steps into the dark. Sometimes he looks back up to the sky with the same eyes that we had.

Flight of the Twilight Species
Kelley Calvert

I landed in Indianapolis unexpectedly, like a bird nudged out of the nest, the ground hurtling towards my face in a bad dream where I couldn't figure out how to use It was the year the Colts became a comedy troupe, the year my father was diagnosed with an incurable cancer, the year millions poured into the streets to pound drums against modern feudalism, the year the six billionth child was born on the back of an overly-extended planet, the year my brother hobbled home from Iraq while America's onward march began skipping like a scratched record, the year I'd have to fly or perish.

Abattoir
Nancy Nicol

Even though the Bible says God gave us dominion over fish of sea, fowl of air,

over every beast that moves, He must have meant In the Beginning, before slaughterhouses or Dolly, before children had pets like my little Valentine.

I know about pets-at-risk and it happened to me in Grade Three. I was Miss Gunnell's favorite even before I made an Iroquois longhouse using real leather. My mother was privately jealous, but I'd seen it come out once before when I gave auntie the clay rabbit I'd made, and not her. And when I got an "A" on the longhouse, my mother reminded me it was sheep skin she'd brought from the tannery.

That same year I saw a red-faced man wearing a soiled apron run out of a windowless barn across Route 9 in front of our car. He chased a sheep that bolted and jumped but got cornered in a doorway. I watched him slam and shoulder her. I saw her look me in the eye, passive, gentle and trapped the same way the man in the news who fled from a cruiser, dug for his keys but was shot dead in his own lobby because he didn't recognize authority, or the meaning of certain words like 'stop.'

I learned the meaning of abattoir first hand and is why I never eat lamb.

Red Peppers
Gloria Nixon John

He is proud when he hands me
three red peppers for roasting
they are a siren in my white kitchen---
his Cheshire grin tell me he knows
the gesture is a mix of gift and imposition.

This is an easy way to please him and so
I slice the pepper in half lengthwise,
remove the pulp and seeds,
flatten them on the grill, turn the broiler to Hi.
the scent is both bitter and sweet.

My mother, dead for twenty-nine years
stands next to me at the stove,
apron around her shoulders like a harness
faded roses climb from a rickrack hem.

I want to tell her to take off the apron
to throw it down, to run from the stove,
but, the truth is I would give anything
to see her standing just as she did.

Once the peppers are charred then cooled
I remove the blackened skins,
the exposed flesh beneath is slack,
moist, more pink than red
like that most private flesh.

I soak them in olive oil and garlic
before I place them on the plate
that mother bought
with S&H Green Stamps,
hold them up as an offering---

He will put the peppers into his mouth
tell me how good they are.

Reaching for God with Feet in the Air
Linda Ann Stelljes

I don't recall the details of the conversation that day—just the immediate effect it had on me. My mother and I had been talking about God. At that young age of eight, it's likely that it was not a heavy treatise on religion. Perhaps, our conversation was inspired by something I heard in Sunday school. The discussion led to where to find God. God lived in heaven and heaven was in the sky.

So how was I to get to God who lived in the sky? I dashed outside to the swing-set in our backyard. I climbed onto one of the swings. Pulling back on the metal chains with my hands, I propelled myself higher and higher. I just knew that if I swung as high as I could with my legs stretched straight out and tipped upward that I could reach God in the sky.

Thinking back on that day, I can still capture that feeling of spirited zeal. I believe that's why my favorite spiritual place to reach God is still outdoors, especially in beautiful nature surroundings. With my feet in the air flying high toward the heavenly blue sky or with my feet planted solidly on the ground, reaching for God I go within.

A Bookworm's Confession
Murli Melwani

The only security in the public library, way back in the sixties, in Shillong, India, was a wizened veteran who made the round of the various rooms, reminding patrons that it was closing time. The security guard missed me ensconced in a comfortable sofa in a corner. I heard him and told myself that I'd leave in five minutes. I lost count of time. The gnawing in my stomach brought me back to reality hours later. In the eerily quiet library, I prowled on all fours hoping that an exit had been left unlocked. I spent a hungry night surrounded by books. The next morning, I waited till there were a fair number of people in the library before I slipped out.

A "library worm" would be a better description.

State of Being
Mari Maxwell

I am only human in this temporary vessel. And I am counting the pieces I leave behind. Today a white eyelash. Yesterday, a wrinkle smiling permanently upon my cheek. Before that a cancerous breast. Then the other, to allay the fears. Each the story of a moment. Each becoming more precious with passing years. Where these days there are fewer in front and more behind. I carry each with pride. Some might say scars, imperfections. I like to think warrior wounds. Signs of living and loving. Evidence this body has carried me and my traumas with dignity, strength and care. Over the decades. Through the joys and pains. Those broken places heal if left to mourn. Rebirth of self and vessel – a richer mixture than what was before. Abandonment strikes deep within – I shed it all.

I tread bolder, with purpose. Thrill at the stray cat bully seeking human touch, the sound of hailstones rat-tat-tatting on the roof, my wee one making birthday muffins to gift a friend. These be only transitory days. To be clutched greedily. Celebrated in abundance. For night will come. With it the silence of a life lived. Loved. Lost. An essence on a wisp of air. No longer touchable. Just was. You. Me. Everyone.

And so I write. Put it down. Ink on page. Thoughts and fears. Permanently sealing I was here. I was. I am. I will be.

Cold Hands, Warm Hearts
Kavita Das

We leave the pizzeria and make our way back home to Union Square. It's not more than ten Village blocks but the night stings of winter and we quicken our strides knowing that each step brings us closer to home and to warmth. My left hand is enmeshed in his right hand, which is nestled in his right coat pocket. It's what we usually do during walks home on cold nights.

I count on him for warmth. I know that no matter how late I stay up reading, writing, or more often watching pointless TV, as soon he feels the mattress sag with my weight, he will turn towards me, his eyes still closed. He opens his arms and his legs to me. My nose finds warmth against his chest while my toes are enveloped between his firm shins. Falling asleep this way is often my last memory for the night.

We walk on with my hand obscured in his pocket. After a while I have to wiggle my fingers to verify which ones belong to me. He's walking quickly and I'm working to keep pace with him, the strides of my five-foot frame much smaller than those of his taller frame. I feel a sense of buoyancy perhaps because we have the sidewalk to ourselves. The Strand Bookstore on Broadway comes into view telling me we're approaching our block. As we take our last steps towards home, I see my breath ahead of me in the air as my ears begin to sting but I know that on this cold night I'll find warmth.

Bowl O'Gratitude
Harriet Riley

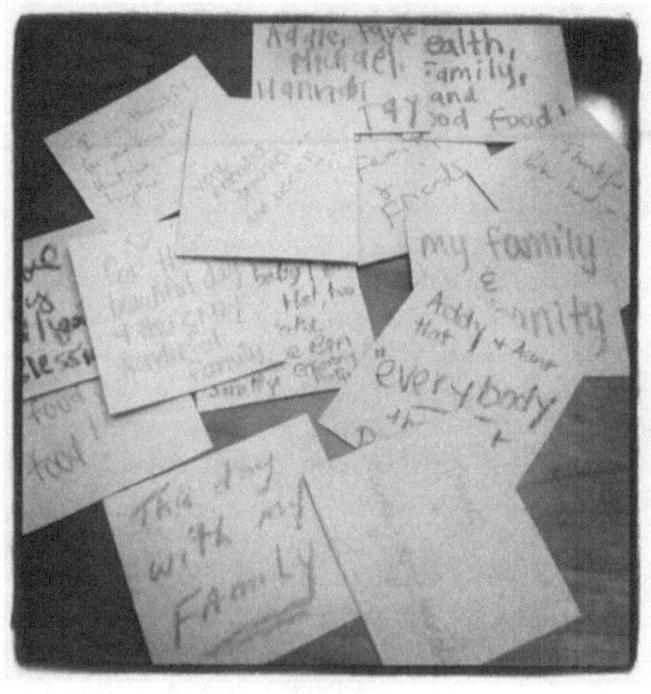

The salt air was wet on our faces. We took turns holding the soft babies in the cool air with the waves bouncing the boat like a seesaw. Deep sadness was just below the surface. But we choose laughter as we gathered on this coastal island.

It was Thanksgiving morning and months before we had sprinkled the ashes of a loved one in these very waters. We were healing in the sunshine, the salt and the people gathered together. Among other family members, I was with my second husband and his daughter by his first wife, his son by his second, and my two daughters by my first husband, now deceased. Not the traditional family, we were in the process of creating our own community to share the time-honored American tradition. What brought us all together was not turkey and salt water, but a sense of shared family.

When we had first arrived at the island house the day before, I had set out a bowl and asked everyone to place in it what they were thankful for this year. These notes made us all think about the good things in our life rather than the losses that were always on our minds. Little Addie, age 3, who had lost both her parents in a plane crash, had me list 12 people and a horse she was thankful for. Her blessings overflowed. One person listed, "Extended families…and beer!" Another wrote, "For this beautiful day and this crazy, wonderful family!"

Surrounded by love and filled with gratitude, it was Thanksgiving at last.

Summer Intern
Laura T. Jensen

He hands me the needle.

"Here, it's your turn," he says.

I glance at the woman in the chair. She cleans the lab and I've been seeing her every day for the past month. A large southern woman, Emma's fleshy arm is propped on the edge of the lab table.

"Come on child, get on with it," she drawls. "Ya'll do jest fine."

She smiles and jiggles her arm almost begging me to inflict pain. Before this, my needle sticks have been oranges. Emma will be my first human stick.

Up until now, I've been quite content to spend my days with my test tubes and smears. Things are different today.

The man in charge of hematology stands at my elbow. Emma sits in front of me, and several of the women from the lab hang back, watching. The cavalry no doubt, ready to step in should I screw up.

With a deep inhale I encircle Emma's arm with the rubber tourniquet, making a small loop to secure it in place. I tap the area in the bend of her inner arm and watch while numerous large veins bulge to the surface. They all looked perfect for sticking.

Uncorking the needle and exposing its sharp tip, I choose the middle vein in the vein field that is Emma's arm. The needle slides in easily and within a millisecond blood begins to fill the tube. I am thrilled. Emma looks up and smiles.

An arm reaches from behind me and yanks off the tourniquet just as blood starts to gush from the end of the tube.

"Always remember to remove this once you've hit pay dirt," he says. "Nice job though."

Emma chuckles and says I look whiter then my lab coat.

The Rider

I was only a child... when I started to cycle
the world was so new and unabashedly wide.

I was the explorer, of mountains and places,
careless and free, towards all that was strange.

I learned how to balance, the line I held,
with the stabilizers I rode, and on we propelled.

But sometimes it was hard, and some were long;
there were times I fell down, when I was not strong.

I succumbed to the worries, of the possible pains,
and tightened the grip, that I held on my reigns.

So seasons did come, and seasons did go,
and the rides of this life, came to have me slow.

In worry and fear, of my failures toll,
for each little stumble; I added control.

And I no longer rode, as valiant or strong,
so I scolded my horse, on account of this wrong.

→

Till one day I found, we were standing still,
and there was the abyss, I saw at my ill.

I had tightened my ropes, in such stiff embrace,
that my horse did not move, held fast in her place.

I was afraid to advance, tired and unsure,
but fearful to stagnate, to die premature.

A glimmer of courage, devised new handles,
but my body was weary, from tensely held hands

Then in an act of blind faith, I released my fears,
I loosened my ropes, a little shy, but sincere.

So I learned how to ride, once more up on high,
first walking, then trotting, then in galloping stride.

You see, we are riders. On wild horses we run,
wide eyed and eager bent, to chase down the sun.

e. Kuether
5. 2014

The Rider
Eric Kreutter

I was only a child… when I started to ride,
the world was so new, and unfathomly wide.

I was the explorer, of mountains and planes,
fearless and free, towards all that was strange.

I learned how to balance, the fire I held,
with the stallion I rode, and on we propelled.

But some days it was hard, and some days were long,
there were times I fell down, when I was not strong.

I succumbed to the worries, of the possible pains,
and tightened the grip, that I held on my reigns,

So seasons did come, and seasons did go,
and the tides of this life, came to tame me slow.

In worry and fear, of my failures toll,
for each little shake, I added control.

And I no longer rode, as valiant or strong,
so I scolded my horse, on account of this wrong.

Till one day I found, we were standing still,
and there was the climax, I saw of my ill.

I had tightened my ropes, in such stiff embrace,
that my horse could not move, held fast in her place.

I was afraid to advance, timid and unsure,
But fearful to stagnate, to die premature.

A glimmer of courage, desired new lands,
but my body was weary, from fiercely held hands.

Then in act of blind faith, I released my fear,
I loosened my ropes, a little shy, but sincere.

So I learned how to ride, once more up on high,
first walking, then trotting, then in galloping stride.

You see, we are riders, on wild horses we run.
wide eyed and eager heart, to chase down the sun.

CONTRIBUTORS

MICHELLE ARDILLO is a Louisiana native known as the "Cajun girl in a kilt", Michelle Blanchard Ardillo is a lifelong reader who teaches middle school English and literature in a suburb of Washington, DC. She is currently working on a middle grade novel about a missing suitcase as well as a series of weekly essays being published on her web site at www.michelleardillo.com.

SHARINE AUPKE is a chef and former food columnist. She is an emerging writer finding her voice again after suffering writers block from a divorce.

JADE BANKS (Jade!) is a writer, book publisher, teaching artist, arts administrator, producer, community folklorist, photographer and author of *On Being Fat, Black And Female*. Founder of Iman Books, she made Harlem history by publishing the *Signifyin' Harlem* literary journal (2002-2004). Jade served as publisher/executive editor of eleven youth anthologies in the NYC School system and publishing advisor for *On Fire!!* literary journal of Rider University. Jade is the NYC Researcher/Coordinator, Curriculum Developer and Trainer for *The Will To Adorn* project of the Smithsonian Institution. She is Director of the Community Folk Culture Program at Mind-Builders Creative Arts Center. She is also a featured interviewee in the HBO/Cinemax documentary, *Cutting Edge*, and was filmed for *Let's Get The Rhythm, Images Of Dignity: Decent People's Children And Blacks In New York*. Her literary and photographic works are archived in permanent collections at the Smithsonian Institution and the Schomburg Center for Research in Black Culture.

VICTORIA BROTT grew up in a small Midwestern town and relocated to Southern California when she was seventeen. She met her husband in Los Angeles during the social revolution of the 1960s. Returning to college as a young struggling mom, she majored in what she loved most: literature. Now a retired high school English teacher, Victoria enjoys her growing family and sharing her lifetime experiences through short stories and poetry.

JAMIE BRUNSON is a poet, award-winning African American playwright, named a "New Voice in American Theatre" by the Edward Albee Theatre Conference and executive director of First Person Arts, a non-profit dedicated to transforming real life stories into memoir and documentary art. Her poetry has been published by Blushing Moon Press in the anthology, *Cape Henlopen Poets 2010*. Her plays have been performed at: the Kitchen Theatre, NYC; New Freedom Theatre, PA; the Harlem Theatre Company, NYC; Walnut Street Theatre Second Stage, PA; Karamu House, OH, Providence Black Repertory Company, RI and Abingdon Theatre, NYC. Her playwriting awards and honors include: a Panelist Choice Award at the Edward Albee Conference for her Blues drama, RED, WHITE & BLUEs and Chesterfield Film Company Fellowship Semi-Finalist (2000). Ms. Brunson holds an MFA from Sarah Lawrence College and a BA from Temple University.

NOTTY BUMBO is a poet, author, and artist living in San Francisco for more than 40 years. His work has appeared in a number of small press publications, including *The Amphigoric Sauce Factory, Writing Without Walls, Kindred Spirits,* and *Poesis.* His poem "Song For The End of Days" will be included in an upcoming collection being published by *Entropy Magazine. Eleven Poems Past and Present*, a chapbook, was published in 2002 by Off Yer Duff Publishing. His first novella, *Tyrian Dreams*, was published in 2014.

KATRENIA BUSCH is a 28-year-old mother of two, and has been working in healthcare for over a decade. She has been published in *Literature Today, The Screech Owl*, Quincy University's *River Run Magazine* and contributes articles on how to improve health care for *Senior Care Quest*.

YUAN CHANGMING, 8-time Pushcart nominee and author of *Mindscaping* (2014) and another 3 chapbooks, is the world's most widely published poetry author who speaks Chinese but writes English. Tutoring and co-editing *Poetry Pacific* with Allen Qing Yuan in Vancouver, Changming has poetry appearing in 949 literary publications across 30 countries, including *Best Canadian Poetry* (2009,12,14), *BestNewPoemsOnline, Cincinnati Review* and *Threepenny Review*.

ANDRES CISNEROS was born and raised in the heart of Caracas, Venezuela. Andrés comes from a family of progressive thinkers, artists, educators and performers. Encouraged from an early age by family, as well as Venezuela's cultural heritage, Andrés became involved in various performances showcasing Venezuelan dance and music styles. Outside of Venezuela, Andrés has lived, experienced and incorporated diverse elements from the Arts and Music of the Diaspora into an evolving career as a percussionist. Andrés currently resides in Philadelphia Pennsylvania, where he teaches and performs as a freelance percussionist and vocalist throughout the Northeast region.

KELLEY CLAVERT In addition to traveling the world with a question mark in hand, enjoys the usual joys life has to offer: coffee in the morning, long, leisurely weekends, live music, and intelligent conversation. When not trying to decide which word goes where, she teaches others about deciding which word goes where. She currently resides in the Golden State in a town that is usually foggy…but next to the ocean nonetheless. You can learn more about Kelley on her website www.KelleyCalvert.com

ELAYNE CLIFT is an award-winning writer, journalist and adjunct lecturer. She is the author most recently of *Hester's Daughters*, a contemporary, feminist retelling of The Scarlet Letter. Her columns appear regularly in the Keene (NH) Sentinel and the Brattleboro (VT) Commons and she is a reviewer for the New York Journal of Books. A Vermont Humanities Scholar, she lives in Saxtons River, VT.

C. A. DAVIS is the author of *Inside Out: Real Stories with Real Meaning* and *My Mother's Genes*. Her writing is based on true events based on family secrets she's exposed in attempt to help others to deal with similar difficult issues. She has been a guest on several television and radio shows to discuss her books. Davis lives in Louisville, KY and creates her own Derby hats each year.

KAVITA DAS is the marketing and communications director of Applied Research Center and Colorlines.com by day and a writer by late night (or by early morning). She writes mostly creative nonfiction and is currently working on a biographical project. Her work has been published in *The Rumpus, The Sun, Thought Catalog,* and *Dash American*. Das lives in New York City with her husband and beloved hound, Gavin.

JEANNETTE DRAKE is a retired psychotherapist (LCSW), poet, essayist, and visual artist offers spiritual guidance nationally and internationally (under a pseudonym) to individuals in crisis. Her writings appear in *Callaloo; Obsidian; The Southern Review; Honey Hush!: An Anthology of African American Women's Humor; The Sun Magazine, Black Magnolia: A Literary Journal;* and *Chickenbones: A Journal,* among others. *Journey Within: A Healing*

Playbook and Promise: Inspirational Fantasies were published in 2005 and 2011. A recipient of awards from the Virginia Commission for the Arts, the Virginia Center for the Creative Arts and the Hurston/Wright Foundation, her memoir, *Far as the Eyes of God Could See*, is under consideration for publication.

CARRZA DUBOSE, PhD is an Assistant Professor at Virginia Union University in Richmond, VA. He holds a B.A. from Fisk University in Chemistry, an M.F.A. in Writing from Spalding University in Louisville, Kentucky; and a PhD from Morgan State University. His areas include 20th Century African American Literature, psychoanalytic literary theory, gender, queer, and masculinist studies. CarrZa is an award winning short fiction writer and has published several critical works. CarrZa is a recent recipient of College Language Association's Margaret Walker Memorial Prize in Fiction, Morgan State University's Graduate Award for Creative Writing, and the Adele Holden Creative Writing Prize.

ASHLEY DURAN is a recent graduate from Bucknell University with a degree in creative writing. She has recently begun the publication process for both her poetry and short stories. An avid writer, with a relentless love for language and culture, Ashley now lives in Paris and is pursuing her Master's in Literature at the Sorbonne.

JUDITH ELLEN is an educator and consultant with over seventeen years experience in the health and human services field. She is the creator of FEISTYWords, a gutsy creative writing and yoga workshop for women and girls. Learn more at www.transcendconsulting.org

MICHAEL ESTABROOK is a recently retired baby boomer poet freed finally after working forty years for "The Man" and sometimes "The Woman." No more useless meetings under florescent lights in stuffy windowless rooms. Now he's able to devote serious time to making better poems when he's not, of course, satisfying his wife's legendary Honey-Do List.

JANE FALLA has been a writer and editor for more than 20 years, and is currently an assistant editor at Smith College. She lives in western Massachusetts with her family.

PAMELA GAY teaches flash fiction at Binghamton University (S.U.N.Y.) She is the recipient of a New York Foundation for the Arts (NYFA) fellowship and a national e-book award for her creative narrative nonfiction collection *Homecoming*. Her work has been published in a variety of literary magazines and two anthologies. Her sentence-a-day project "Moments of Being" can be viewed at www.365sentences.com

LARRY GODWIN taught at Oregon State University and the University of Montana, from which he has retired. His self-help psychology book, *Surviving Our Parents' Mistakes*, was published in 1999. His work has appeared in *ByLine, the Journal of Outsider Poetry*, and *Montana Voices*. He lives in Missoula, Montana.

MARYANN GREMILLION'S first micro essay was published in *The Sun* magazine in October 2010. She teaches creative writing to children and adults. She also collaborates with other artists on both collage and writing projects. Her work has appeared recently in local studios and galleries in Houston, Texas, where she lives with her husband and a chubby cat.

PAUL HADELLA teaches at Southern Oregon University and has worked as a freelance writer for many years. He lives in a little white house on the corner of Talent Avenue and Joy Drive with his wife, daughter, and three cats.

GERALD HARRIS is president of the Quantum Planning Group where he specializes in assisting businesses and organizations in a wide range of planning tasks. Gerald received his BA in economics from Morehouse College, where he graduated Magna Cum Laude, and an MBA in finance and business economics from the University of Chicago. He has published for several publications, most recently in the June 2013 issue of *Strategy and Leadership*. Gerald is the author of *The Art of Quantum Planning, Seven Ideas from Quantum Physics for Breakthroughs in Creativity, Innovation and Leadership* (Berrett-Koehler 2009), published worldwide including Brazil.

DAH HELMER's photographs appear in American Photo, Mondo 2000, The Best Of Photography 2001, 2002, 2010 (Serbin Publications), and on several book covers. Dah's creative focus is mainly on writing poetry, with his fourth book, *The Translator* (Transcendent Zero Press) published in 2015 — Google: dahlusion

JENNIFER HIGGINS is a graduate of the Gerontology Ph.D. Program at the University of Massachusetts. Results of her studies have recently been published in the *Journal of Aging and Social Policy and the Journal of Aging Studies.* Over the course of her academic career, Dr. Higgins has conducted policy analyses and participated in numerous research projects and she was invited to join other experts, gambling clinicians and academics for the purpose of designing the first senior problem gambling diagnostic tool.

SHIRLEE SKY HOFFMAN is a retired marketing consultant who lives in Chicago, IL where she now has the time and energy to devote to her lifelong addiction to writing.

GIUSEPPE INFANTE is a poet, writer and educator from Brooklyn, New York. He earned a B.A. in English and an M.F.A in Creative

105

Writing, both from from Long Island University Brooklyn, and won the Esther Hynemen Award for Poetry in 2012. He is one of the founders and managing editors at Overpass Books (overpassbooks.org) and The Otter (ottermagazine.com). Several poems of his are published in *Brooklyn Paramount, Poems by Sunday*, and *visceral brooklyn*, among other journals and magazines, and in his first collection, *ways of dying naked in mexico city* (Overpass Books, 2012).

JASON IRWIN grew up in Dunkirk, NY and now lives in Pittsburgh, PA. He has an MFA from Sarah Lawrence College. His first collection, *Watering the Dead,* "won the 2006/2007 Transcontinental Poetry Award and was published in 2008 by Pavement Saw Press. *Some Days It's A Love Story* won the 2005 Slipstream Press Chapbook Prize. His poem "Main Street" was nominated for a Pushcart in 2005. His one act play *Civilization* had its staged reading debut on April 24, 2010 at The Living Theatre, NYC. "Undone" a one man/one act play was performed at the Willits Shakespeare Theatre as part of Scripted: an Evening of Original One Act Plays.

LAURA T. JENSEN is a published writer of creative nonfiction. She is a member of the NC Writers' Network and her works have appeared in, for example, *The LA Review, A Long Story Short* (story of the month 6/2011), *OneTitle Magazine, The Foliate Oak Literary Magazine*, an anthology *Lessons From My Parents*, and she was a finalist for the Eric Hoffer Award (Best New Writing 2013). A New Jersey transplant, she is a resident of NC.

ANIKA H. KLIX is a Human Resource professional and freelance writer and editor. She earned a MA in Organizational Leadership from Gonzaga University and a BA in Sociology from Washington State University. She is currently working on a biographical novel about her ancestry's migration from Northern Germany to America in the early 1900's and is editing a non-fictional novel written by a life-long friend. She resides in Seattle, WA with her three children, Cody the hyperactive Cavalier Spaniel, and Maliea the Persian cat.

VANESSA MALLORY KOTZ is a writer and editor living in Baltimore Maryland. She covers the arts, culture, and her unusual personal experiences.

ERIC KREUTTER lives and works in Eastern Africa with a vibrant community in the field of youth leadership development. Eric was raised in this part of the world, where he now resides in Kampala, Uganda, with his beautiful wife Dani, and newborn son, Leo. Eric's creative writing is a search for beauty in the human process of becoming – the journey towards meaning, fulfillment, and purpose. More of his poetry and creative work can be found on: www.BecomingBeauty.com

MICHELLE LEGAULT lives in Minneapolis, MN where she spends her days managing the office for a local water softener company. In her spare time, she writes short stories, photographs everything within eye-shot and blogs about her adventures on the site www.minnesotalegaults.blogspot.com. Her photography is forthcoming in the literary journal Kansas City Voices.

JING LI lives in San Francisco and is a devoted and dedicated teacher now at Raoul Wallenberg High School where she founded the Chinese/Mandarin Language Program. She was also a finalist for the California Jack London Writing Contest in non-fiction.

SUSAN MAHAN has been writing poetry since her husband died in 1997. She has written four chapbooks and has been published in a number of journals and anthologies. She has been an editor for the *South Boston Literary Gazette* since 2002.

JAS MARDIS (Jas. Mardis) is a long-term resident of Dallas, Texas. He is an awarded poet, radio commentator and storyteller with current projects that include anthology editing, quilting, radio and print commentary and coordinating workshops and genealogy start-ups and reviews at *The Family Story Project*. Jas. has been awarded The Pushcart Prize for Poetry. He has also received multiple GRIOT awards from The National Association of Black Journalist/Dallas Chapter, for radio commentary. In 2014, Jas. Mardis was inducted into The Texas Literary Hall of Fame.

MARI MAXWELL has a forthcoming poem in *Veils, Halos and Shackles International Poetry Journal on the Abuse and Oppression of Women*. Mari's work has featured in *Poetry 24, A New Ulster, Crannog, Boyne Berries* and other online and print publications in the USA, Ireland and UK.

MURLI MELWANI lives in Plano, TX and is a guest columnist for The Dallas Morning News. Melwani is the author of *Stories of a Salesman*, a collection of short stories *Deep Roots* (a 3 Act Play), and two books of literary criticism *Themes in Indo Anglian Literature* and *Themes in the Indian Short Story in English: An Historical and a Critical Survey*. He taught English Literature at Sankardev College Shillong, India. Melwani's short stories have been published in magazines in various countries and nominated for a Pushcart Prize. A few have been included in anthologies, including *Stories from Asia: Major Writers from India, Pakistan and Bangladesh* (Longman Imprint Books, U.K). He is also a playwright and the author of a collection of short stories: *Stories of a Salesman Writers Workshop 1967*.

JASMINNE MENDEZ is a performance poet, actress, teacher and published writer. She is a graduate of University of Houston where she received both her B.A. in English Literature and her M.Ed. in Curriculum and Instruction. Mendez has performed her poetry in venues all around Houston, including the MFAH, Rice and the Alley Theatre and has shared the stage with respected writers and poets. Mendez has been published both nationally and internationally and her first multi-genre memoir *Island of Dreams* was released in 2013 by Floricanto Press. She is currently at work on her second memoir *Thick Skinned*.

NICOLE L. V. MULLIS is the author of *A Teacher Named Faith* (Cairn Press). Her work has appeared in literary magazines, anthologies and newspapers. Her plays have been produced in New York, California and Michigan. She is a Robert J. Pickering Award for Playwriting Excellence winner and a Gertrude Stein Award finalist. She has been a *Battle Creek Enquirer* columnist since 2006.

BONNIE J. MORIS, PhD is a professor of women's studies, on the faculty at both Georgetown and George Washington University in Washington, D.C., and the author of nine books--including three Lamnda Literary Award finalists *Eden Built by Eves, Girl Reel, Revenge of the Women's Studies Professor*. Her most recent book is *Women's History For Beginners*, and was introduced on C-Span Book TV. Morris is a scholarly advisor to the National Women's History Museum planned for the D.C. mall.
Visit www.bonniejmorris.com.

NANCY NICOL grew up in Jersey City and commuted by bus and train for eleven years to Manhattan, where she attended Friends Seminary. During those daily, repetitive journeys as a child, she composed poems and short stories—in her head. Several years ago she began writing things down and her first publications, "*Dirty Work*" and "*Too Late Daughter*" were published in *Roll: A Collection of Personal Narratives* (Telling Our Stories Press, 2012). She has been a featured writer and artist on *Cape Women Online Magazine* where she is a regular contributor. She is a collagist, printmaker and oil painter and is currently working on a third draft of her first novel. Nancy lives in Wellfleet, MA. See www.nancynicolart.com

GLORIA NIXON-JOHN holds a B.S. and M.A. from Wayne State University as well as a Ph.D. from Michigan State University. She has published academic articles, essays, poems, and short fiction in both small, mainstream presses and e-zines. Among them, *Clover, Dunes Review, Gemini, The Language Arts Journal of Michigan, The Prose Poetry Journal, Telling Our Stories Press, Wayne Review, Women on Writing,* and *The English Journal.* She has chapters in *Those Who Can Do, Teachers Writing, Writers Teaching, Writers in The Classroom*; and *The Women of Country Music,* and upcoming in *To Light a Fire* (Wayne State University Press). Her longer work includes a literary biography of Canadian poet Bronwen Wallace and a novel entitled *The Killing Jar,* based on the true story of one of the youngest Americans to have served on death row. Her memoir, *Learning from Lady Chatterley,* will be published in 2015.

HARRIET RILEY is a free-lance writer focusing on non-fiction articles and short fiction. She is a writer-in-residence in Houston middle schools with Writers in the Schools. She has taught undergraduate writing classes at the University of West Florida in Pensacola where she lived for eleven years before moving to Houston. She's also worked as a non-profit director, hospital marketing director and newspaper reporter. She has her M.A. in print journalism from the University of Texas at Austin and her bachelor's degree in English and journalism from the University of Mississippi.

KATHLEEN SAVILLE is currently on faculty at the American University in Cairo (Egypt) where she teaches academic and creative writing. She is working on a memoir project about her years as an ocean rower with her late husband Curt Saville. She has recently published stories in Adventum, a literary magazine of outdoor adventure writing and Vermont Magazine while completing her MFA in Creative Writing from Stonecoast MFA program.

JUDITH SERIN teaches literature and creative writing at California College of the Arts and lives in San Francisco with her husband, Herbert Yee. Serin's collection of poetry, *Hiding in the World*, was published by Diane di Prima's Eidolon Editions, and her *Days Without (Sky): A Poem Tarot*, seventy-eight short prose poems in the form of a tarot deck with illustration and book art design by Nikki Thompson, was published by Deconstructed Artichoke Press. She writes fiction as well as poetry, and her work has appeared in numerous magazines and anthologies, including *Bachy, The Ohio Journal, Writer's Forum, Nebraska Review, Woman's World, Colorado State Review*, and *Barnabe Mountain Review*. Most recently she has published prose poems/memoirs in the anthologies *Proposing on the Brooklyn Bridge* (Grayson Books), *When Last on the Mountain* (Holy Cow! Press), and *Impact* (Telling Our Stories Press); in the journals *The Paterson Literary Review, First Intensity, Paragraph*, and *the blink*; and in a chapbook of nine prose poems, *Family Stories* (Deconstructed Artichoke Press).

ROBERT M. SHAFER grew up as a Chicago slum boy and an abandoned child. Those early years inspired most of his writing. He served four years in the U.S. Navy, with two and a half of those years aboard warships. He worked thirty-five years as a film/video editor in San Francisco and spent five years as a ranch hand, caring for horses. He currently resides in Northern California.

S. F. SIDDIQUI was born and raised in the Washington, DC area, and returned to Maryland after earning a BA in English from Amherst College and an MA and MS Ed from the University of

Pennsylvania. After several years as teacher and English department chair in local high schools, she now teaches writing at Montgomery College and is developing her own fiction and nonfiction prose. She lives in Maryland with her husband and two children.

LAURENCE SNYDAL is a poet, musician and retired teacher. He has published more than 100 poems in such magazines as Columbia, Caperock, Lyric and Gulf Stream and in many anthologies including *The Pagan's Muse* and *Visiting Frost*. Some of his work has been performed in New York City and Baltimore.

LINDA ANN STELLJES is both a literary and visual artist. As a journalist, her news and feature writing articles were published in various publications. Her work as a visual artist include book arts, collages, drawing, mixed media, watercolor and pen and ink. Linda is an active member of Houston's Women in Visual and Literary Arts (WiVLA). Some of her works have also been published in the WiVLA monthly on-line newsletter. She collaborated with eight other artists to create a pop-up book with the Houston Book Arts Guild in response to Hurricane Ike, which was also exhibited at Sandy Gallery in Portland, Oregon. She finds therapeutic writing to be a valuable tool in counseling. She takes some of her inspiration from existentialist Rollo May.

DANIEL STONEHIRSCH has been writing since she was digging holes on the Jersey Shore, and graduated from Washington University in St. Louis with a B.A. in English Literature in 2007. She is currently living in Washington, D.C. where she is the Program Director for a non-profit which engages youth from across America in service to the homeless and hungry of D.C.

FRAN TEMPEL was born in Montana, lived in California and New Jersey before finally settling in upstate New York State with her husband. As a teacher Fran has always taught her students the value of keeping a journal and how their lives are worth documenting. Telling stories about her past helped her to discover the person she is today.

DAWN MARIE THOMPSON is now a freelance writer and editor living and working in Oakville, Ontario, Canada, following a long career in the world of advertising and corporate communications. Having some years ago published The Twenty Foot Apartment, a book of prose poetry, she has over time become committed to the flash format. Now approaching her eighth decade of life, she is currently working on Before I Forget; a memoir of sorts, but packaged as a collection of flash non-fiction essays and stories she describes as "shards of memory." Under the Peonies is one such shard.

VINCENT J. TOMEO has been published in the New York Times, Comstock Review, Mid-America Poetry Review, Edgz, Spires, Tiger's Eye, ByLINE, Mudfish, The Blind Man's Rainbow, The NeoVictorian/Cochlea, The Latin Staff Review, and Grandmother Earth (Vii Thru XI).

SUSAN WHITE, originally from middle Tennessee, received her master's degree from the Bread Loaf School of English and her MFA from Stonecoast. She teaches high school English in Asheville, North Carolina. When she's not grading or writing, Susan enjoys running on the mountain trails with her five dogs. She has published short stories and personal essays in Front Range Review, River Walk Journal, Diverse Voices, Barely South, Pisgah Review, Deep South, The Battered Suitcase, and the anthology *Dear John, I Love Jane.*

CARL WHITEHEAD, JR is a native Baltimorean who loves the music of Sinatra, Cooke and Coltrane.

CRYSTAL WILKINSON is the author of *The Birds of Opulence* (forthcoming from University Press of Kentucky, 2016), *Water Street* (Toby Press, 2002), which was nominated for the Orange Prize and for the Zora Neal Hurston/Richard Wright Foundation's Legacy Award in Fiction, and *Blackberries, Blackberries* (Toby Press, 2000), which was named Best Debut Fiction by Today's Librarian Magazine. Crystal is writer in residence at Berea College and a recipient of the Chaffin Award for Appalachian Literature. She is also a recipient of the Sallie Bingham Award for the promotion of activism and feminist artist expression. She and her partner Ron Davis are the editors of *Mythium: A Journal of Contemporary Literature Celebrating Writers of Color and the Cultural Voice* and owner of *Wild Fig Books*. She has been published widely in anthologies and literary journals.

ABOUT THE EDITOR

As a lifetime diarist, CoCo Harris is drawn to personal narratives. For years she has guided others with crafting personal narratives through creative writing workshops and various memoir projects and publications. Her story began in Atlanta, GA, and has traversed the Washington DC Metro area; Nigeria, West Africa: Seattle, WA; Louisville, KY; The Coast of Georgia; and Central Pennsylvania's Susquehanna Valley. Though she now lives in central PA, CoCo is particularly at home anywhere sun and surf meet. She is the Founding Editor of Telling Our Stories Press.

CoCo Harris is constantly exploring the notion of how we tell the stories of our lives with both fiction and nonfiction

www.ingramcontent.com/pod-product-compliance
Lightning Source LLC
Chambersburg PA
CBHW020703260626
47157CB00008B/3112